THE WOLF

Standing alone
Brave and sure
Sending it's fierce howl
Thru the still night
Its strong sleek body
Illuminated by the moonlight
As it runs easily and endlessly
Independence shining in his eyes
Knowing quite well
He is the king of his domain
Willing to take on any challengers
Who questions his dominance
You may see him running with the pack
Or roaming by himself
But always using the keenness that he has
To live on, wild and free

EARTHBOUND

I hear the call from above
So I turn my head up to the sky
I see the eagle
Flying all alone
Something stirs deep inside of me
Could it be the sign of independence and freedom
That I know the eagle possess
Or its piercing call
That sends shivers thru my body
Oh how I wish I could be up there
Gliding in and out of the clouds
Flying around for hours
Sending my own call to those below me
I feel my spirit becoming restless
Longing to break free
From this force that holds me down
I sense the eagle staring at me
And I stare back
I can see the mocking look in his eyes
For he knows I am bound to earth
I yell to him
That someday I'll join him
In his endless flight of joy
I'll be there, flying besides him

Flying among the clouds
Soaring ever so high
I sit and stare
The restless feeling inside
Reminds me of
The eagle
Inside us all

I see the eagle
Flying above us all
It is smiling
For it knows
It has something
We have not

COME FLY WITH ME

I want to spread my wings
Feel the air rustle thru my feathers
Carefree and happy, I can be me
Flying in and out of the clouds
Dipping down low
To catch the rays of the sun
I am free, wouldn't you like to be
Come join me, do not fear
Release your burdens, release your worries
And come fly with me
No deadlines, no commitments
Time stands still up here
So come fly with me
I will guide you thru the mysteries of the sky
Show you mountains shrouded in mist
The morning sun, just beginning to rise
I will help you feel the cool breeze
As it ripples across the lake
So come fly with me
And you will never forget the peace and serenity
Of soaring across a clear blue sky
So won't you please
Come fly with me

A bright moon
Against a pale sky
The eagle soars
Flying high
He is happy
For he knows
He is free

THE EAGLE

Black and white
Soaring ever so high
Among the clouds
Sending
Its sharp and piercing call
To all that care to hear
Flying with the wind
It is carefree

My eyes dimmed
For the moon shone
As though it was broad daylight
I stared motionless, breathless
Unable to move
As though I were in a trance
A calmness over settled me
The sight I beheld
Was most unbelievable
The shadows from the wolf
Were sleek and smooth
As he glided
In front of the moon
The shadows of the eagle
Soon appeared
Soaring across the moon
At the time the two shadows crossed
I again heard
The howl of the wolf
And the cry of the eagle
My senses sharpened
My icy bones soon warmed
My frayed nerves mended
And my battered soul, healed

In the stillness of the night
I heard a howl
Very distinct, ever so clear
It sent a chill thru me
That soaked every bone
I then heard the cry of an eagle
Piercing the solitude
And shattering my nerves
I look around for support
And my frightened eyes
Caught a glimpse of the iridescent glow
From the moonlight
I turned round full
To bask in its light
And soothe my weary soul

INDEPENDENCE AND FREEDOM
{THE WOLF AND THE EAGLE}

Its eyes sharp and piercing
Soaring, dipping, gliding
Freely thru the sky
Traveling for miles
On a single breeze
With no special place to be
No deadlines, no commitments
No one to please
Just pure, simple, and free
It spots its shadow below
Prowling thru the underbrush
Stalking, hunting, roaming
Its sleek agile body
Glistening in the moonlight
As its eyes shine fierce and independent
His confidence radiating
He knows he can stand alone
For he is a survivor

WINTER

The deceptive sun shines bright
Radiating its beauty
Off the glistening powdery white snow
There is a coldness in the air
That all can feel
People hurrying to get home
Or someplace warm
A place to hide
From the snowflakes that fall
And the howling wind, that makes you shiver
The frozen toes, and runny noses
I surely believe
That winter is here

A CHILDS FIRST SNOWFALL

The snow is falling outside
White and powdery
So very fine
I long to touch it
Yet I fear it's too fragile
And I will crush it
I love to stick my tongue out
And catch the snowflakes as they fall
Snowball fights with my friends
And building snowmen too
And maybe if I'm really lucky
A day off of school

A FALL DAY

The sun shines bright
The clouds roll lazily
Against the still sky
The sound of the birds chirping
Is a music that relaxes my soul
A gentle wind begins to blow
Sending a rustle
Thru the golden leaves
I lean back against the tree
And enjoy the peace of it all

SUMMER

The bright glistening sun
Radiates off the clear blue sky
The warmth and happiness
That builds inside
When a gorgeous summer day arrives
A gentle breeze, that whispers thru the trees
It's a perfect time to get away
To be by yourself, or with friends
Maybe sit under a big tree
Shaded by the leaves
Maybe you'd prefer to walk around barefoot
Feeling the blades of grass
As they tickle your feet and toes
There is nothing better than summer
For it reminds you of that feeling
That you got when you were young
And you knew summertime was near
And nothing could remove the smile from your face
When summer is finally here

It starts as a seedling
And grows into a beautiful flower
Its petals begin to sprout
So very soft and fragile
Such a pearly white
A thing so full of beauty
In a world that can be so cold
It is these small wonders
That we must learn to cherish
So don't be in such a hurry
Take the time for things that matter
Remember a friend you have ignored
Think of the last time you called your mother
A kind deed you did for a stranger
Whatever it may be
Always remember
To stop and smell the flowers

STARLIT NIGHT UP NORTH

It is immensely quite
The noise of the city
Has vanished
I stand alone, gazing upwards
At a million stars
As their radiance
Beams down upon me
I breathe deeply
Enjoying the pure, unadulterated air
As it cleanses my soul
Such an awe inspiring feeling
Those tiny stars behold
I reflect on how
Peaceful, tranquil, and comforting it is
To relax underneath the sky
Illuminated by the starlit glow

MOONLIT NIGHT

In the quiet of the moonlight
I turn troubled eyes
To the stillness
Answering my cries
I am searching for a calmness
A settling of my thoughts
And a soothing of my soul
The tranquility I have found
Underneath the moonlit glow
Has done wonders
For my bothered mind
For nothing seems quite as peaceful
Than taking a stroll
Thru a path
Illuminated by the moonlight glow

AN EVENING SWING

The different shades of hues
Blend together so perfectly
Almost a though they were painted
The evening stars
Send a heavenly twinkle
Across the dusky sky
A gentle breeze
Slightly swings the hammock
Lulling me to sleep
To the quiet evening sounds
In the backdrop

In the early morning mist
Something stirs
I know not where
Some quiet spirit
In the air

A MOUNTENOUS MOMENT

The world lays below me
The worries and troubles of it
Cannot reach me here
I am engulfed by beauty
And embraced by sunshine
I stretch my hands to the sky
And enjoy the pillowy softness
Of the clouds
As they drift through my fingers
A gentle breeze
Rolls across the mountaintop
Rustling my hair
And broadening my smile
Oh, sweet escape
If but for a few hours
It's a break, a relief
From the hectic world below

THE FORGOTTEN SHELL

Clear and blue
Endless in its capacity
The waves roll
Strident and strong
Towards the shore
Where they dissipate
Into piles of foam
And then recede
Back into the depths of the ocean
But all is not gone
When the waters roll back
For upon deliverance of each wave
A new shell is carried
To be left upon the sand
Some have remained where they have floated
Others are washed back into the waters
While some are picked up
By those passing by
Who still cherish and recognize
The beauty and uniqueness
In something as simple as a shell

THE OCEAN

Pounding and pulsing
Like a heartbeat throbbing
Crashing and booming
Recklessly against the rocks
So deep blue in color
Yet so vividly transparent
It follows no direction
Only its own path
So subtle and smooth
Yet ever so powerful
It can float you out to nowhere
In just a flash
Or suck you under
And make you disappear forever
The beautiful music
That the waves make
Like an orchestrated symphony
As they wash over you
Like a calming gentle rain
One can stay fixated
On the tranquility of the ocean
All day

PURE INNOCENCE
{THE RISE OF DAWN}

It's a cool late evening
Pure and quiet
The leaves crackling gently
Underneath my soft footsteps
The noise of the hustle and bustle
Of everyday life gone
I am alone, yet not lonely
A light breeze envelops me
As I gaze upwards
At an ever lightening sky
I breathe deeply
And let a peacefulness settle over me
As I bask in the early morning glow
Have you ever seen pure innocence
I have

CREATION

It starts with a heartbeat
And grows from there
A face begins to form
With ears and a nose
And we must not forget
The fingers and toes
How such a small fragile being
Can blossom from seemingly nothing
A life growing inside
Waiting to be born
To venture into the world
And see all that is new
Such a miracle it is to see
A life develop before me
But before we even know
It will be grown

BABY

The skin so soft and gentle
The tiny fingers and toes
So very small and fragile
The rosy cheeks
And the fuzzy hair
The comfort you know is felt
When you hold them close
Such a gentle being
Nothing else is as precious
You want to wrap your arms around them
And never let them go
The worlds worries seem to melt
When you're surrounded
By a baby's love

GROWING UP

Life gets so confusing
And hard to figure out
I'm growing up so fast
What's it all about
Things are changing quickly
Time is flying by
I'm becoming a different person
Sometimes I wonder why
At times it gets real scary
And I want to run away
But I know things will fit together
Somehow sometime someday

GETTING OLDER

The years are passing by
Like leaves in the wind
Friends long gone
Only fond memories to reflect upon
No longer in the rat race
Life goes at a slower pace
The wisdom gained thru the years
The triumphs and tears
But now it's time to move on
And you will be dearly missed
When you are gone

PARENTS

They stand by me
And support me
When I falter
They are my extra set of footprints
When my feet are to heavy to walk
They embrace me in their warmth
And shelter me
From this cold cold world
Their love protects me
From the evil that lurks
They are always there
To dry my tears
And partake in my laughter
They give me guidance
And teach me values
So that I may share this with others
They are my bond
That holds me together
In times of need
They have made me
Who I am today
For this I thank them
For the reflection of me
That I see in the mirror
Is them

DAD

Someone who is there
To offer guidance and support
One who is always willing
To lend a helping hand
One who helps you
Understand your problems
Without passing judgment
Someone who is there
Everyday for you
Someone who possesses
An unconditional love for you
That is true and true
These are the traits that I find in you
That I cherish and value too

A MOTHER

A person that you can rely on
When you need someone there for you
Someone who will listen to your problems
And try and help you with them
A person who is there
When you need love and caring
And to dry away your tears
Always there with a kiss and a hug
When you are hurting
Someone who always seems to know
Exactly what you need
So always keep your mother
Close to your heart
And always remember
To thank her in some way
And not to take for granted
All that she does for you

MOM

The bond between you and I
Is so very special to me
I cherish all the moments
That we are able to spend together
If you had not come into my life
I would have felt
So incomplete
You taught me
That it's okay to love and care again
I can't begin to tell you
How much you mean to me
I always hope
That I can always be there for you
Just like you are for me
Thru the tears that we have shed
And the laughter we have shared
Have made us best of friends
So on this special day
I want to let you know
How much you mean to me
I love you so much
Not just on mother's day
But every day, thru and thru
And I am blessed that you are my mom
And am so thankful
That I have a mom like you

A SISTERS LOVE

Being able to form a friendship
That has lasted thru the years
Is a memory
That I'll always cherish
The closeness that I feel
When we are together
Like a bond that can never be broken
I can confide in you anything
We shed tears together
And laughed with each other
But most importantly
We shared together
You are always there
When I need you the most
Or just a little
Someone who's love
Is unconditional
And what I value most
Is being able
To call you my sister

A SPECIAL KIND OF LOVE

The feeling you get
When you're with each other
A closeness that can only form
Between two people, that understand each other
For who they are, not what they are
A bonding that grows over a period of time
An undying love that cannot be broken
No matter what
The respect you feel for each other
Can never be lost
You're able to confide in each other your troubles
Without fear of being judged
You've been there together
To smooth over the rough spots
And keep each other laughing and smiling
You've discovered in each other
Something that is so very dear
A special kind of love that can only be found
Between two people
That care so much about each other

BEST FRIEND

There's a certain feeling I get
When I think of you
It's an emotion that fills me with happiness
I recall the love and caring
That passed between the two of us
The fun times we shared together
And the tears we shed together
We were inseparable
I will always cherish these memories
That I have of you
And if someday I lose all that I own
I will still have the memories
Of the times we had together

A TRUE FRIEND

When we need to talk
Or need a friendly face
We know we can turn to you
If we need somebody to support us
Or a shoulder to cry on
We know we can turn to you
A person who will help set us straight
To talk to us even if we don't listen
We know we can turn to you
To listen to our problems
And give us advice
We know we can turn to you
A person to help guide us
Thru life's trials and tribulations
We know we can turn to you
A person who is always there
When you need them most
We know we can turn to you
For you are a true friend

At times it feels life is not worth living
Everyone keeps taking all you've been giving
The days and nights are full of sorrows
And there's no wish for any tomorrows
No one seems to understand
And few offer to lend a helping hand
But those who do
Are friends that are true
They'll stay till the end
Helping your broken heart mend
The key is to never give up and begin to try
Say see you later, but never good-bye

TURN TO ME

When your world is unsure
And you feel you will falter
You can turn to me
I am strong
Like the roots of a tree
My shoulder is there
When the tears begin to fall
My arms are always ready
For a much needed hug
When the world seems cold and empty
Search for me
I will embrace you
And fill you with warmth
When you are frightened
I will be there
Like a beacon in the night
Scaring away the demons
And shining bright
When you are feeling all run down
Turn to me
For I will give you the boost
That is needed to carry on
And always keep in mind
That no matter where you may be
You can always turn to me

MEMORIES

Laughter fills the air
Along with the chatter of voices
People telling their stories
Not one is alike
Talking, sharing, and laughing
They talk about their life
The good times and the bad times
The fun that they had
Their adventures, misadventures, and friendships
Oh how dear they are
The many memories we all have

FIFTY YEARS OF MEMORIES

A bond was formed
Some fifty years ago
It started with two kids
That had found a love that flowed
If one had said it wouldn't last
Let them look at the fifty years gone past
A family was born and children raised
For this task let them be praised
And don't forget the chore
Of running seven corners hardware store
Or the summer vacations at paradise resort
Back in the days when Chisago city
Was mostly remote
And the trips to the cottage in white bear
That became quite an affair
For come summer time
They closed the house in highland
And doubling the size of their cottage
Was their new plan
Now thru all this we must not forget to mention
About bringing aunt jean and uncle Morris
To our attention
For if we all take a moment to hear
The words uncle Morris most feared
As aunt jean stood on the deck and yelled
Morris come in Morris come in
And no matter how far across the lake he cruised
He always knew when fishing time was thru
Now this is only a glimpse
Into the past fifty years
For a poem would turn into a book
And a book an autobiography
If we tried to capture all the moments
Of the last fifty years
Let me sum it up by saying
There were times of tears and uncertain fears
But the love always remained thru the years
For there was plenty of laughter that was shared
As there always is between two people who care
So I congratulate these two kids
Who played it quite smart
And formed a marriage
That began at the heart

Dedicated to my grandparents Shirley and Ronald Freeman 8-18-96

Never let go of your dreams
Your hopes and desires
For one day they will come true
Your dreams are important
For it is something that no one can take away
You control what becomes of your dreams
Do not let them slip away
For they are an important part
Of our daily existence
For where would we be today
If everyone had decided
That their dreams were foolish too

HOPE

Despair not
Though you have been lost awhile
For there is a place
That's shining bright
So even on your darkest nights
Try to keep in mind
The sun will always shine
The moon will gleam
And the stars beam
So keep your head up
Never let it falter
And when you begin to stumble
And feel you'll never rise again
This is when you need to find the strength
To grasp the hope
That is hiding in failure

CHANGE

There is a time
In everyone's life
When you feel a little unsure
A little scared of what the future holds
But you must not let this fear hold you back
You must continue on your way
Confronting what blocks your path
And taking on the challenges
That would be easier to avoid
You must never let this mystery get you down
Keep an open mind
Remember that there is hope
When all you see is despair
There will be times when you feel you can't make it
That you don't want to take that first step
But you must go on
Though it seems quite hard
Or all your strength and energy
Will be drained from you
So even though it's scary
You must go with this mystery
That no one can predict
But all know so well
And that is the mystery of change

HELPING HAND

Good-bye my best friend
I have given you up for a new trend
No more nights will I spend with you
My life has begun anew
The road ahead is bumpy
Forgive me if I may seem grumpy
It's a long journey to travel
Very rocky, just like gravel
Yet I know I'll pull thru
With a helping hand from you
If you would be so kind
And help me out of binds
Stand by me
No matter what may be
I feel I have the strength
To go that extra length
For I know I'll pull thru
With a helping hand from you
Sometimes I feel so low
Like getting hit by a heavy blow
I know from the bottom I must climb
To rise above the grime
Yet there are days when each rung seems steeper
And I feel I'm plunging deeper
Yet I know I'll pull thru
With a helping hand from you
One day at a time
What a rhyme
Yet it rings so true
For an addict who has the blues
Yet I know I'll pull thru
With a helping hand from you

Day by day
Living in a haze
Couldn't deal with it anymore
Needed something to cover up
This messed up life
Gone too far
Far beyond anybody's reach
Living on the edge
Of reality and fantasy
Then without really knowing
What has happened
The edge falls away
And into fantasy we fall
Not sure when we'll return
Can't believe it came to this
What happened
Whatever it was
We'll never be the same
We've gone back to the thing
We know will help
To ease the pain, hurt, and suffering
Wishing the haze will never end
But knowing that it must
Or we'll be lost forever
My cries of help
Buried underneath it all
Does anyone hear anything, anything at all

WASTED

Drifting further and further
Feeling good, feeling fine
Gone on a journey
A journey of endless time
Turning glazed eyes
To things only you can see
As you drift in and out of your daze
There are no thoughts of any kind
And you know through the haze that has formed
There's no sensation to compare with this

FAST RIDE

You've gone for a fast ride
All the houses flying by
Is it time to die
The pedal is to the floor
Your friend is glued to the door
Traveling at such a fast rate
Life is in the hands of fate
Feel the pounding in our ears
Can you hear can you hear
The end is drawing near
Do you feel any fear any fear
Time to live time to die
My friend has begun to cry
Let it go let it go
It's the end of the show
The tires are spinning
My friend is grinning
The road ahead is clear
Have another beer
The car is going at the speed of light
There is no more fright
Time to laugh time to laugh
We are out of gas
The show is over
We are sober

Oh, life is so dear
I think I'll have another beer
My body has begun to rot
Time for another shot
Pass the herbs
Watch out for the curb
Do not worry
We are not in a hurry
We'll make it there in time
If someone has a dime

SNAPPED

Thoughts swimming around in your head
Your feelings are a blur
Nothing seems to make any sense
You aren't thinking straight
Feeling as though you're going crazy
You want to rip out your mind
And put it back
When it's all settled down
It's scary as all hell
When this occurs
For you're not sure
Quite what's going on
Have I lost all control
Completely flipped out
You scream inside of yourself
Please somebody save me
And bring me my sanity back

IN MEMORY OF SETH COLIN MANLOVE
NOVEMBER 4TH 1971- MARCH 11TH 1991

Help me forget today's pain
Stop my tears that flow like rain
I long to see your face
To fill that empty space
A hole deep within my soul
That seems to grow and grow
No more hellos no more good-byes
Your future plans gone awry
Suicide denied your right to live
What a loss, you had so much to give
Your face still so vivid and clear
A close friend to all, you were so dear
The memories of you shall never die
For all the tears I cry
They call your name
Reminding me
That things will never be the same

CHEATED

Another young life
Stolen from us
Why it had to happen
I am unsure
All I know, is what I see
Going on around me
The pain, sadness, and hurt
The shock
Of such a terrible and tragic deed
They say
God taketh and god giveth
Why must it be
There is so much suffering
One cannot help but think
Spare my friend
And let it be me

THE ROLLERCOASTER OF LIFE

End over end we tumble
Down into the darkest of tunnels
Falling head over heels
Into the bottom of the bottomless caves
Plunging our way into the unknown
And then without warning
We come to a sudden halt
This is the mystery of life
Turning, twisting
And then suddenly peaceful
Then it starts
All over again
Without ever knowing
When it will stop or start
And so we take life
With the utmost care
And try and keep the surroundings peaceful
For as long as possible

STREETS

Growing up on the streets
I have seen a lot of things
I have been broken and battered
Yet never defeated
Many a people I have met
And lasting impressions they have left
My innocence and youth destroyed
Values and beliefs lost
Sadness was swallowed
And turned into anger
There were days when I pondered
How my life
Would never be the same
For one is irreversibly changed
When one has to struggle
To survive

HEAVY SHOULDERS

There are days
When the world drags me down
The weight of her problems
Seeming to weigh heavy
Almost crushingly
Against my weary shoulders
I cry out in frustration
And wonder why me
Just when it seems
I'm about to be swallowed
And left to drown in my self pity
Pictures flash before my eyes
Depicting those I have met
So less fortunate than me
With greater worries and concerns
And I notice that their shoulders
Are stooped and slouched forward
That is when I realize
The pressure upon mine
Seems not so heavy
For I begin to look at the advantages
And not the disadvantages
Of my situation
The burden of my shoulders
Is now less restricting
Allowing me more room
To help shoulder
The problem of those
Worse off than me
And as I do so
I see their shoulders
Start to straighten

JUST LIKE US

You pass them everyday
Without a second thought
You see them lying in doorways
Or on the street
With a sign for help
Others just sitting
With a vacant stare
If they are acknowledged at all
It is with a look of contempt
They have been called
Beggars or bums
Worthless humans
Rotting our society
You think to yourself
Why should I give them money
Or a friendly passing smile
For you think they're not worthy of this
But maybe you should take
The time to think
That they are still a person
They need to know
They are still worth something
That someone would care
If they were hurting inside
And they would be missed
If they happen to die
So maybe it is worth
Some of your time
To let these people know
They are not just some derelict
Roaming the streets
They share a common bond
For they are people
Just like us

JUDGE US NOT

Do not judge us
By the clothes we wear
Do not judge us
By the friends we have
Do not judge us
By the length of our hair
For it doesn't matter how we look
Or who are friends are
It is how we think how we act
And the knowledge that we possess
That makes us special
We may not fit in your social circle
Or enjoy being with your friends
But do not judge us
For you do not know who we are
Only what we are
In your eyes
We are young and immature
But do not judge us
For young we may be
But immature we're not
You say wisdom comes to the old
Well do not judge us
For we have wisdom equal to yours
We are looked down upon
But we are young and a new generation
We are the future so before you judge us
Judge yourself

They say
Trust is a must
But we've learned the hard way
We will have to live
Without that must

We're asked to trust people
Who have no trust in us
We're asked to believe in
Those who have no faith in us
They are unable to understand
Why we can't
Relate to them
They speak to us
As if we know nothing
About the world around us
If only they understood
What we've seen
What we've been through
If only they knew
Then maybe they could
Comprehend with us

Days fly by
They all seem the same
Full of sorrow, full of joy
Will we ever be able to see
Thru our tears
And find that laughter
That's somewhere out there

We are young at heart
But yet,
We feel ever so old
We've seen so much
Our innocence destroyed
We are unable to find the joy
That once was there
It's hard to hang on to
The drive that keeps us all going
We were so young and vibrant
Whatever happened to those days

Is it too late
To forget how to hate
Anger building inside
It's too hard to decide
What of our fate
Is it to late
We hear everybody say
That we can't change our way
But little do they know
We are still able to grow

BURDENED

What is this burden
That weighs upon our weary soul
Its drained us of
What energy we had left
It buries us in our sorrow
And takes away our joy
It drags us to the edge
And watches
As we slowly fall over
Just to grab us
And pull us back
To live thru the pain some more
Will we be able to survive
What seems to be a hopeless mess
It doesn't seem possible
But we know we must try
Or all our strength will be lost
To the despair and desolation
Of this burden that weighs upon us
Can this burden be lifted
Oh, how we hope so
For we cannot go on like this
The burden of problems
That have been pushed deep down inside
But refuse to go away
And the memories that surface
With the slightest trigger
That we thought we had blocked out
Now do you know of
The burden we speak about
It is the burden of life

THE ACCIDENT

One can only smile so long on the outside
To cover the frowns on the inside
Eventually the sadness takes over
And when the tears are dry
The anger explodes
You are still in denial
Thoughts racing thru your head
That this didn't happen to me
And all will be fine
Yet there comes a time
When reality
Slaps you in the face
It wakes you up
To face your situation
When all you want to do
Is pretend it doesn't exist
You want it all
To return to the way it was
When life was fun and good
You long to be
Happy and an able bodied healthy person
Once again
If only you could turn back
The hands of time

DEPRESSION

I long for my tortured soul
To find its inner peace
My emotions brewing and building inside
Like a tea kettle ready to explode
A blanket of sadness
Wraps itself around me
And will not let go
The endless stream of tears
Rushes like a river
Drowning out the laughter
I yearn to hear
My days and nights
Seem one and the same
I see no end
To this weary game
I stare with empty eyes
At the figure in the mirror
All I see is a shell
Of what used to be me
I hope someday, I shall return
To the person I used to be

THE PROTECTIVE WALL

Life has become
Beyond our reach
We've built a wall
Protecting us, shielding us
From the pain
Of knowing our feelings
Have grown numb
From each risk
We have taken
To love to care to trust
Someday we'll break thru the wall
That surrounds us all

BEGIN AGAIN; LIKE A CHILD

There are no footsteps
For me to follow in
No one for me to lead
No one for me to lag behind
I choose my steps carefully
Almost as though I were a child
Learning to walk
I close my eyes to what I've seen
And open them anew
With the curiosity
Of a blind man learning to see
I could find no escape
From the life I led
No matter how I tried
The past and present
Continued to collide
Dimming the future
It is then I understood
Running or hiding
Would not shelter me from this life
I so badly wanted to start again
A clean slate, a fresh start
I searched in vain
To find a way
To cleanse my soul
And awaken my spirit
I finally realized
The answer to my quest
Laid within the children
They saw things we were blinded to
Heard things that fell deaf
Upon our closed ears
And most importantly
They saw life as it could be
Not as it was already formed
Before them
It is on this path
Thru the eyes of a child
I have begun life again

THE FRAGILE CHILD

The memories still haunt us
From our tragic childhood
How our innocence
Was stripped from us
We had to grow up
Way to fast
We were never given the chance
To enjoy the beauty of life
We grew up with the knowledge
That love was shown
Thru abuse and neglect
That is what we lived
We had to act grown and mature
We were forced into acting like an adult
When all we wanted was to be a child
We were deprived of feeling love, caring, and happiness
Still today we find it hard
To be able to show these feelings
Life wasn't easy
Growing up in a world
That didn't seem to care about us
We will never fully recover
From this unspeakable damage
That was done unto us
But we must try to remember
That we don't have to take on the struggle
Of unburdening our minds, and freeing our souls
Of our terrible past alone
For there are still those around us
Who strongly believe
That there is good and kindness
Left in all of us

IMAGES

Beyond this place of tears
There shines a brilliant place
Of dreams and desires
As I reach out
It falls thru my hands
For it is only an image

THE DREAM

I had a dream one day
I dreamt of a world that I lived in peace
Where black and white went hand in hand
No wars against our brothers and sisters
No tears to be shed by the parents
Of lost sons and daughters
A time when a disagreement
Could be solved thru compromise
Not from an exchange of bullets
No longer would our children fear each other
And the people are able to come out
From behind their locked doors
When will the world realize what they have done
Destroying generation after generation
Thru the horrors of war, prejudice, and violence
This tragedy must come to an end
If anyone is to be spared
So I plead with you now
Share with me this vision, this dream
Of a better place for all

A DREAM DESTROYED

The world had finally learned
That what they had been doing
Had destroyed all possible dreams
Of the world being a decent place
To live in, to grow in
Now that they have realized that
We can finally live in a world
That we can all feel safe
And at peace with everybody
Too bad it's only a dream
Only a dream
But maybe we'll live to see the day
The dream turns real

TO HONOR, TO OBEY, TO SERVE

When you see the flag unfurled
Do your eyes mist over
Does your body go rigid
Taut with the pain that the flag brings
Memories of childhood, friends lost forever
Who died for the stars and stripes
Do you ever wonder, if it was all in vain
How much longer can we bear
To hide behind the falseness and the lies
How many more of our children must die
Before we decide to give peace a chance
Can we keep justifying the slaughter
Of the young, the old, the innocent
How many memorials must we build
To remind us of the damage, and the death we wreak
When will enough be enough
When will we realize that no one wins in war
How many more lives must be lost
Before our debt is paid

WON'T BE FORGOTTEN

The people who tried to change the things
That were not right
Will not be forgotten
The blood that was shed
And the tears that fell
Will not be forgotten
They were honored
They were disgraced
But they will not be forgotten
There were those who believed in them
And those who didn't
But they won't be forgotten
For they changed the ways that weren't right
They fought and died for what they believed in
But they won't be forgotten
For their memories and spirit
Lives on with us

THE LAND THAT FED A NATION

The paint on the farmhouse
Has begun to fade and peel
The tractors and plows
Lay lifeless in the fields
The smell of grandmas hearty breakfast
Have been replaced with
The overpowering stench of must and neglect
The huge barn that looms overhead
Now stands empty
The sound of the cows mooing
The clanking of the milk pails
And kittens frolicking on hay bails
Have all vanished
The only thing that greets me, is dead silence
That reverberates thru the empty barn
And hits me hard
As I continue on my way
I walk thru the cornfields
Noticing the scarecrow
Who once seemed so brave and sure
Now hangs limply on a stick
A threat to no one
All this I can bear no more
It seems like we do no longer care
For those who sweated their blood and tears
Will we continue to avoid
Offering a helping hand
To those that helped our nation flourish
And toiled the land
That fed a nation

They who began this wrong
Will rue the day
When they ordered teenagers to obey
Now we are pledged to win
And rebellion will be our way

I have seen you before
Yet you don't recognize me
Do you not recall who I am
I walk in your shadows
And appear in your dreams
I foresee your future
And know your past
Are you still wondering who I am
I am the figure you see
Off in the distance
I am the chill that's in the air
I am always with you
Yet I am never there
Are you confused yet
Let us delve a little further
I am your best friend
Though we've never met
Who am I
I am the side of you
That you deny exists
The side you never want to see
Yet I will be with you
Till the end of time

There was death at every door
And hell at one dark window
With eyes that burnt like fire
At those that looked
And those that dared
Were grasped by deadly terrors
And then
As the heart began to beat
He smiled
For he knew his work
Was quite complete

I am the master of my fate
No matter how deadly the game
My will is unconquerable
Because I am
The captain of my soul

The walkway shone with a bright light
Hiding the child from the dark night
No one to cling to
So far from home
The child has begun to roam

THE NIGHT

The shadows on the wall
Move around like a bouncing ball
Under the covers the child goes
All you can see is his toes
The boogeyman is near
You can sense the child's fear
There is nowhere to hide
He longs for his mom by his side
He prays for the night to end
For he knows daylight it will send
The child begins to scream
In runs his mother
And tells him it's all a bad dream
On her way out, she turns on the light
Protecting the child from the night

LIFES ROADS

Cruising down the road
Cities flying past me
Miles rolling by
I know not what lays ahead
Not quite certain what I've left behind
I feel the sun setting behind me
And see the future shimmering ahead
I hear the spirits calling
From the still starry sky's overhead
And I begin to smile
And not to worry
For I know the road I choose
No matter which way that may be
Whether traveled or untraveled upon
Will be one filled with new discoveries
For it is a road yet untraveled
By me

STREET MUSICIANS

When summertime is here
You can hear them everywhere
The beginner on the sidewalk
With his guitar case open
Hoping to make a buck
Or the entire band
In the park jamming
Hoping that one day
They'll see their name
Up on the billboard lights
Whether just starting out
Or well rehearsed
I love to hear the street musicians
My ears are perked
To absorb the beats
That surrounds me
I feel the pulse of the city
The sounds all grooving together
Sending a vibe thru your body
That regenerates your soul

MEANT FOR MY SOUL

Rock and roll
Was meant for my soul
The beat of the drums
Loud and bold
The guitars are wailing
And the lead vocals
Are singing it out
Turning up the radio
To hear my favorite song
Hoping it lasts long
Yeah, I'll tell it to you again
Rock and roll
Was meant for my soul

CITY BEATS

Do you hear the music
Can you feel the power
Let it move you, consume you
It's time to rock, time to roll
The party is near
The night time air is clear
People moving, people grooving
Hustling here and there
Cruising down the street
With the window down
The sounds envelop you, grab you
You feel so energized
Can you feel the pounding pulse
Surrounding you
The city is alive

THE RAT RACE

In such a hurry
To get to work
Can't be late, too much to do
Trying to remember, to hug the kids
On your way out the door
Your brain is spinning
Trying to figure out
How to balance
All that you have to do
Wondering what to have for dinner
Maybe it's better, to just order out
Who has the time anyway
To sit around the table
Making a mental list
Of what your day encompasses
How did we ever let
Our life get so hectic
We have forgotten about
The simple pleasures of life
Everyone's in too much of a haste
To get it all done
Maybe if we try, just a little harder
We can find the time
To remember to slow down
And not let life
Be nothing more
Than a deadline

WHEELCHAIR BOUND

It's strong and sturdy
And keeps me steady
When I'm weak and wobbly
My legs, now replaced by wheels
Spinning, turning, churning
But getting nowhere
I want to escape
But I am a prisoner
Chained to this chair
It controls where I go
Who we see, what we do
I wonder if someday, I will be free
To roam, to wander, to explore
By myself, on my own
No chair haunting and controlling
My every move
Just my legs
Spinning, turning, churning
Getting me everywhere

A cool gentle breeze
Rustles thru the trees
You ramble on
Without a care or worry
On your mind
You're totally relaxed
As you breathe in
The pure unadulterated air
You continue to stroll
Thru the peaceful and serene beauty
Of a back country road
You wish this journey
Would never end
Yet reality sets in hard
And you realize
You must return
To the concrete walls
Of the polluted city

A TRIBUTE TO TWIN CITIES CATERING HOLIDAYS

Twas the night before Christmas
And all thru the kitchen
We were cooking and baking
And moaning and bitching
We've been here for hours
We can't stop to rest
This rooms a disaster, just look at this mess
Tomorrow we've got 3000 people to feed
They expect all the trimmings
Who cares what we need
Are feet are both blistered
We've got cramps in our legs
Patty just knocked over a bowl full of eggs
There's a knock at the door
And the telephone's ringing
Frosting drips on the counter
As the microwave is dinging
200 pies in the oven, desserts almost done
My cookbook is soiled
With butter and crumbs
We've had all we can stand
We can't take anymore
Then in walks Jim, spilling brandy on the floor
He weaves and wobbles, his balance unsteady
Then grins as he chuckles, the manhattans are ready
He looks all around and with total regret, says
What's taking so long
Aren't those orders out the door yet
As quick as a flash, Rachel reaches for a knife
He loses an earlobe, she wanted his life
He flees from the room in terror and pain
And screams
My god woman, you're going insane
Now what was patty doing
And what was that smell
Oh shit it's the pies, they're burned all to hell
She hates to admit, when she makes a mistake
But she put them on broil, instead of bake
What else can go wrong
Is there still more ahead
If this is good living, we'd rather be dead
Lord, don't get me wrong, we love holidays
It just leaves us exhausted

All shaky and dazed
But we promise you one thing
If we live till next year
You won't find us pulling our hair out in here
We'll hire another cook, a baker, and a pasta maker
And if that doesn't work, we'll call another caterer

The river rolls endlessly
Following its own path
Bound by nothing
Just like a restless spirit
The trees bordering the river
Whisper secrets
Into your ears
You are calmed and settled
By the rhythms
Of the river

THE MONSTER

I am struggling
Trying to win this battle
For my life
I want to regain my balance
On this uneven pavement
That they call life
Yet I am unable to find
The even keel, that I seek
For depression is suffocating me
And constantly pulling me down
I want to break away
From its nasty grip
For one day, hopefully soon
I will regain my freedom
From the evil monster
That haunts me

COMET; MY CAT, MY COMPANION

I passed her one day
As she lay trapped in her cage
She reached for me with her paw
Our eyes met and locked
I knew then, that this would be
My companion for life
I made her a promise that day
That I would always be there
To love, feed, and care for her
She in turn spoke to me with her gaze
And showed me she offered in return
An unconditional love, that was undying
So through my hardest days
And even longer nights
She is always by my side
Giving a soft comforting purr
In return I offer her my all
A special treat, a scratch behind the ears
A snuggle that only we can share
And thru the passing years
A special bond has formed
And for this I would trade nothing
Yet forfeit all

B-BALL

Round and firm
The bright orange ball
Molds perfectly to your hands
You move effortlessly down the court
Quick and sleek as a cougar
The pounding of your feet against the floor
Is like a rhythmic beat
As you glide in and out of players
Floating by them in a blur
Almost as though in a trance
You sense the basket nearing
Automatically your arms begin to arc
Your feet leaves the floor
The body perfectly poised
The eyes slightly closed
The ears are perked
Yearning to hear the sweet music
And then, there it is
Loud and clear
Reverberating through your body
Swish
A direct hit

NURSES

A tireless job
That never ends
A devotion that only a few possess
The endless tasks
And special little touches
That go unnoticed
Praise that is not given enough
To those that work so hard
To make sure we are comforted
And all our needs met
It is to these hardworking people
That I can't say thank you
Enough

Don't begrudge the past
Grow from it
Don't dwell on the future
For it's uncertain anyway
Bask in the present
For it's what you have
And keep in mind
Life doesn't come with a guarantee
So live each day to the fullest
And always remember
If you can't laugh at life
There's no point in living it

When it's easier to frown
And be completely down
Try to remember those
That are worse off than you
When it seems life can get no more painful
And you wonder why you
Try to remember those
That are worse off than you
When you don't feel
Life is worth living
Try to remember those
That are worse off than you
When it seems the sun will never shine
And your skies are always gray
Try to remember those
That are worse off than you
When you feel you can't find the strength
To carry on one more minute of your day
Try to remember those
That are worse off than you
When you're in dire need of a smile
And a great warm hearty hug
Try to remember those
That are worse off than you
And share with them an embrace
So that it may seem
There's someone else worse off
Than the both of you

I AM STRONG

When life gets you down
And you have no more fight left
Dig in deep
And pull yourself up
Though you may be questioning why
And think there is no point
For you'll just be knocked down again
You must climb to your feet
As many times as it takes
For if you stay down
You will be smothered by the weight
Of life's unbearable burdens
So rise, and rise again
For you are a fighter, a survivor
And you will not be beat
By life's curveballs
For you are a strong person
And you shall overcome

Some say I am lucky
To still be among the living
To have survived such an awful accident
I should be thankful to still be alive
Yet they don't know or feel
The constant pain and suffering
I endure each day
My independence and freedom
Ripped from me without a care
Confined to this horrible wheelchair
No longer a purpose
Do I feel I have on this earth
Wondering why I am still here
A productive member of society
I am no more
No longer able to contribute
Anything I feel is worthwhile
I try to remind myself each day
That there are those worse off than me
Yet this thought no longer consoles
Only tortures me
I yearn for the life I once had
Wondering if the day will ever come
Where I will once again be me

SET ME FREE

The sadness and hopelessness envelops me
Like the sun on a cloudy day
I no longer can bear
To be despondent any more
I long to break free
From the ever crushing and suffocating depression
That crashes down on me from all sides
Weighting me down like wet concrete
My life has been ripped from me
The thoughts racing thru my head
Like a never ending tornado
I am no longer living, just existing
I yearn to laugh and share with others
Yet happiness I can no longer find
Only despair and loneliness
I long for the world to release me
From this constant day to day emotional hell
For I cannot fathom
Having to live another day

WORLD OF TEARS

My eyes are blinded with tears
Streaming down my face
Plummeting like a waterfall flowing
No more happiness do I feel
Only enveloped by sadness
That smothers me like a wool blanket
I struggle to break free, break out
From this crushing weight
That bears down upon me
Longing to reach thru to the other world
Where eyes are dry, and smiles broad
Yet no matter how far I stretch and reach
It slips thru my grasp, and I tumble back
Into the world of tears

Chillin out on unit 30
With my homies and my girlies
Seeing a lot of familiar faces
Of all different races
Definitely need a smoke
And that ain't no joke
Hoping to bust out soon
If I can avoid capture by the goons
Need to fly this coop
And get out and shoot some hoops
Once I be hittin the streets
My mustang will be bumpin the beats
Free once more
Time for me to endlessly soar

Jenn likes her two nns at the end
On this she will not bend
If you spell it with only one
She'll come completely undone
Don't mess with her on this
Cause she'll get quite pissed
And always remember she's tough
And things can get quite rough
So when you put the pen to the paper
Make sure you add the two nns
And sign the waiver

FROSTYS RIDE TO THE BIG HOUSE

I'm shackled an locked down
Chains rattling is the only sound
White t-shirt, blue jeans
Was my disguise for the gangsta lean
It's now all been traded in
I'm headed straight for the pen
No more rappin, no more rhyming
All I see is homies dying
Frosty the dope man
Is headed straight to the can
Thought I could hustle a little blow
The fuzz surrounded me like snow
Figured I might as well, take a few of them out
It weren't no ten round bout
Let the clip in my nine fly
Dropped five of them guys
Now looking at 25 to life
With nothing left to give, except some strife
Yet don't count Frosty down
Minneapolis is his town
And with one loud shout
Frosty's busting out

HIDDEN BEAUTY

Gazing out the window
At the falling snow
So heavenly, pure and white
Watching as the hues of the evergreen
Change to pearly white
Drifting back to a time in my mind
When a snowfall was so stressless
Pure and innocent, such as a child
The worries of sliding into a snow bank
Have melted clean away
Only having thoughts now
Of gliding and conquering down the biggest hill
So as the years pass you bye
And you sprout from child to adult
Please don't lose sight
And let your breath still be taken away
By the mystical beauty and awe
Of a magical snowfall

FRIENDS TILL THE END

We met as strangers
To me you were so kind
A friendly smile
A warm hello
Our friendship began to grow
It blossomed like a flower
In the throes of growth
Our small talk soon replaced
No more chit chat
It was time for all night calls
I began to know you were the one
Who would be there for it all
Never to leave me hanging
All bent and dangly
Dependable and reliable
Trustworthy and kind
Only would an ultimate betrayal
Bring our friendship to the end
Yet for this I do not worry
For strangers we were in the beginning
And best of friends
We now shall be
Until the eternal end

FAMILY

Mom, dad, sister, brother
When these words are spoken
Does it instantly bring a smile to your face
And a pull on the strings of your heart
Or does your face begin to grimace
As you fight back the tears of rage
Welling in your eyes
A family connection that can be so strong
Or shattered in just an instant
Is your bond formed simply by name
Or an undying love that cannot be restrained
Do the pictures relive such vivid warming moments
Or are the pages of your album blank
Days that never pass without a phone call
To share that special event, or a quick hello
The time is always there
For the precious trips, that are shared thru the years
A family dinner, that needs no meaning
A special hug or kiss
For no particular reason
The comfort of knowing
They will always be there
For laughter and heartache
Thru momentous and minute moments
Believe me when I say
Words cannot express enough
How blessed and fortunate I am
To be able to state the following words
I have a family
Do you know of what I speak
Are you also
One of the lucky ones

FOR MOM- MOTHERS DAY

When I utter the word mom
My heart fills with warmth
For I think of what that word encompasses
Pictures of you flash before my eyes
And a smile broadens across my face
I think of the times we have shared
And the tears we have shed
All the times I needed you by my side
You were always there
So strong and supportive
Giving me the strength to carry on
I cannot express enough
All the love you bestow upon me
Completely selfless and needless
You always put me first
You carry me through my hardest times
And give me the courage to push on
I will never be able to repay
All that you do for me
But I know that a smile
A simple phone call
And a hug to say I love you mom
Is payment enough

FOR DAD-FATHERS DAY

When I think of what I've learned from you
I cannot help but smile
The values that you instilled in me
That make me the person I am today
And for this I am so proud
The love and compassion
That I always feel in every hug from you
The guidance and support
You have given me thru the years
That have helped me stand on my feet
And survive thru some pretty tough times
A world that can be so troubling
And tough to figure out
Yet I knew I would never get lost
Not with a father like you
For all that you have done for me
And continue to do thru to this day
Is something I can never repay
Yet I know by standing tall
Showing kindness and fairness
And practicing everyday
All that you have taught me
Will be payment enough
So thank you for being that special dad
That every daughter needs

MY SISTER; MY BEST FRIEND

The warmth and happiness
That envelops me, when I think of you
All the special moments thru the years
That we have shared together
And made us so close today
A bond that has grown so strong
Never to be broken, only strengthened
To know I can always rely on you
Through those troubled days and nights
Is a value in you, that I hold so dear
Such a kind hearted, caring woman that you are
Always putting others first
And making sure you are always there
To comfort and console me
For this I cannot thank you enough
And all the little things that you do for me
That mean so much
And go such a long way
For this I can never repay
Yet I will count my blessings every day
And give plenty of thanks
For I know you are
Only a phone call away
And to have you in my life
Has answered all my prayers
And as I think of you
And all you encompass
A smile broadens across my face
For I think to myself
Having a sister like you
Is more than one can wish for
And simply put
Just great

As I hold your hands
And gaze into your eyes
I feel the love so strong
That has remained true
And has never wavered
So as I stand here before you today
I eagerly await those words
Uttered to me thirty years before
And as tears of joy fill my eyes
I whisper back to you
I would be honored to be your wife
And stay with you, thru the remainder of our lives

THE WALL

I once had a heart, that was ever so cold
A solid concrete wall, that no one could penetrate
Not only protected me, yet also shut me off
From the love and warmth of the world
This is the existence that I lived
Feeling safe and secure behind my wall
Little did I realize, how much I was missing
Thinking I needed to love and trust no one
That life would be safer that way
Never did it occur to me
That it would be alright to let people in
Until I met that one person
Who changed all that I thought
Little by little I let pieces of my wall chip away
And let the warmth of friendship
Stream in like the rays of the sun
And thru the crumbling of my wall
I soon realized the world
Was not as callous and cruel
As I once believed
And with a little trust and faith
I was able to soften my heart
And shatter my restrictive wall

THINGS THAT MATTER

A crisp autumn day, leaves scattered around
The pure fresh cleansing smell in the air
A casual gathering of friends
Spending the day, chatting away
The warmth and love that is felt
When your family surrounds you
The smile that broadens your face
When you make another's day
Window rolled down, wind in your hair
The perfect song on the radio plays
As you drive with no particular destination in mind
It's the little things in life, that mean so much to you
And may mean nothing to someone else
You don't let this fact, make you forfeit
The things that matter most to you
For your life can only be lived once
So cherish what's closest to you
Keep it near and dear your heart
For in just a flash
It can all vanish, in the blink of an eye

CLOSE TO YOUR HEART

One meets many acquaintances in life
Yet true friends are few and far between
And can be counted on your fingers
These friends are the ones
You can always count on
They never question or wonder why
They are always there
Before you even have to ask
And through all the trials and tribulations of life
They will always be by your side
These are the friends
You will never fear of losing
So, just like a necklace
Keep them where they belong
Close to your heart

GONE COLD

My world has become routine
No feeling left inside
No longer am I living, just existing
Emotions long gone, except for anger
Just frustration and bitterness
Filling me to the brim
No room for warmth and happiness
Only an iciness fills my veins
A steely droplet falls from my eyes
The coldness in it, freezing the flowers
Suffocating and deadening all scent and beauty
That I so long to enjoy
As despair spreads across my face
I reach out to touch the petals
They shred and fall through my fingers
Just like the pieces of my life
Oh how I yearn to rise above
This dreary existence
That has become so common place

WATERY DREAMS

The rocks are jutting out everywhere
The waves banging angrily against them
Just like my emotions
Pounding away at my body, trying to bust out
I'm searching in vain
For a calmness to wash over me
Like a beacon shining brightly in the night
I feel like a tiny ship
Being tossed around at sea
Flailing helplessly against the giant waves
Just when I feel I shall drown
My head bounces to the surface
And I gasp endlessly for air
Just to be sucked back under again
I struggle with all my might
To break free from the waves grasp
Yet it won't release me
No matter how hard I fight
As I plunge under once more
I wake with a start
Drenched in sweat, not seawater
As I come to, I realize I'm not in the ocean
Just drowning in a pool of my own thoughts and troubles
As I try to drift back to sleep
A thought creeps across my mind
How similar the two are
The battle of the ocean, and the battle of life
All we are trying to do, is survive and not drown

REVITALIZE MY SOUL

My life is torturous
My soul feeling battered
In desperate need of some relief
Who will come and save me
Give me the overhaul I so desire
I long for the rays of sunshine
To bathe over my body
And ease my creaking old dusty bones
I feel my spirit getting restless
And I know what I yearn to see
To get me thru one more arborous day
I crank my neck toward the sky
Straining with all my might
Just to catch a glimpse
Of what I know will cleanse me
Inside and out
And then, there it is
I feel the flapping and beating of the wings
As it pulsates freely above my head
At first the jealousy fills me from head to toe
Yet that emotion is quickly erased and replaced
With a sense of release and healing
I shield my eyes to gaze some more
And what a sight it is to behold
I am fixated
As it glides endlessly and easily
Across the royal blue sky
I have been saved, at least for today
I hope I will at least last a few more days
Until I see the eagle
Soaring freely once again

The gathering of friends
Does so much for a despondent soul
Isolation becomes that much tougher
When you find you have friends that care
A simple card game, that becomes so much more
When accompanied by the gentle sounds of laughter
That helps draw you out of your shell
And makes you yearn to share
In the happiness that is felt
Your thoughts running rampant, in your beleaguered mind
Slowly start to drift away
As you're occupied by the gentle jabbing
Of friends that are helping
Without even knowing the healing impact
They're having on your weary soul
As you say your good-byes
Your shoulders feel a little lighter
For your burdens were raised just a bit
And you know the night will be
Just that much more tolerable
Due to the cheer that was spread this evening
So smile just a bit
And score one for yourself
For at least for tonight
You have outwitted, the tricky battle of depression

HAPPY BIRTHDAY

A time to celebrate
Your joining of the world
Blessing all with your presence
A day to reflect
On your triumphs and tributes
A remarkable day to remember
All of those you have touched
In such a special way
May this warmth that envelops you
On this joyous occasion
Carry and follow you thru
Until that next magical moment
When your day of arrival returns

DREAMS

Your anticipation builds
As the night draws near
You eagerly await
The arrival of sleep
For then it will be time to escape
Into the world of fantasy
Where will you travel tonight
Who will you see
The possibilities are endless
That is the joy of dreams
It is a time to allow your creativity
To escape and roam free
As you feel your eyelids getting heavy
A smile creeps across your face
For you know
The fun is about to begin

The love that is felt between all
Is a bond quite irreplaceable
A special place in our hearts
We have reserved for one another
The smiles and laughter that is shared
Sometimes without a word being passed
These are our special times
That I know I will cherish forever
You both have touched my life
And brought meaning and hope back into it
I can only hope I have returned the favor
At least in little bits
With you both I can share my troubles
And not worry about being judged
Just given a friendly ear and some gentle advice
I know when a smile is needed
It is only a phone call away
So please with the utmost love
I would like to say to the both of you
How blessed a person I am
To have an auntie and unc
Like the two of you

Suicide is the solution
To absolute confusion
I had made no gain
In trying to ease my pain
I was full of hurt and shame
No one tried to help
They thought I was playing games
So I'm giving up the fight
I feel I have the right
I could not go on with life
And I killed myself with a knife
Maybe one day you'll understand
Why suicide seems so grand

CONNECTION

When you find that right person
You connect like a plug to a socket
Your heart fills with warmth
Like the sun soaking thru your body
A lifetime you know you will spend
Just like the eternal stars in the sky
A lifetime of secrets you will share
A knowing that belongs to only the two of you
Your tears will run as one
In harmony your laughter will reverberate
And in many memories you shall share
The bond that you two possess
Shall keep you both united
Until the spiritual end

The days I spend without you
make me so very blue
you brighten up my day
and chase away the clouds that are gray
always a smile you have for me
never sad you let me be
so I wanted you to know
how much you've helped me grow
I send you lots of hugs and kisses
and many a fond wishes

Another sleepless night
You stare at the clock
As time ticks away
You glance back at the clock
Your restless night
Is almost over
Yet, how you long
For the fluffy pillows
That envelops your head
The cool sheets
Draped on you
Like a fine satin blouse
You snuggle under the comforter
Bringing it up to your nose
You feel safe and protected
As you drift off to sleep
A faint smile
Comes across your face
It must be a good dream

CPSIA information can be obtained at www.ICGtesting.com
Printed in the USA
BVOW07s1227240614

356785BV00001BA/15/P